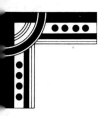

MIAMI VICE SCRAPBOOK

BY JEANETTE FRIEDMAN

COLUMBUS BOOKS
LONDON

CONTENTS

Printed and bound in Italy

ISBN 0 86287 257 X

First published in Great Britain in 1986 by
Columbus Books Limited
19-23 Ludgate Hill, London EC4M 7PD

ACKNOWLEDGEMENT

The publisher appreciates and wishes to thank the NBC staff for its assistance in the preparation
of this edition of the *MIAMI VICE SCRAPBOOK*.

Photo Credits: Juanita M. Cole: 6,7,20,24,25,26,29,59
NBC: 3,8,10,11,12,21,28,30,31,43,46,55,56,57,60.
Warner Bros: 19. Ron Galella: 27,44,45,47,48,50,51,52,53.
DMI: 43. Scott Downie: 44.
Color Photo Credits: NBC: 5, 16, 34, 58. Juanita M. Cole: 14, 15, 29, 32, 49.

Editor: Mary J. Edrei
Cover and Book Design: Mark H. Scala
Research Asst.: Denis Siri

INTRODUCTION

Miami Vice has been featured in every national magazine you can think of, from *Time* to *Playboy*, from *Rolling Stone* to *Tiger Beat*. The adjectives used to describe it are hot, sizzling, sexy, art deco, original, unusual. Critics level it with scathing remarks about shallow cops, pretty violence, and loud music.

Miami Vice received 15 Emmy nominations the first year it was on the air. It did so because it was original. It was the first TV series to spend a fortune on maintaining feature film-like quality, the first to use contemporary music in a way that integrates it into story lines, the first to allow a black man to make very passionate love on prime time television and the first to use a formula of bright, bright colors to depict the seamier side of life. It's also dizzyingly action-packed and a great escape.

By the time its second season rolled around, *Miami Vice* was ripped off by other networks with imitations. Why? Because the *Miami Vice* formula is an advertiser's dream, attracting a young crowd that likes to spend money, and it keeps them home on Friday nights. The hunger for information about the show and its characters is so great, it seems that people just can't get enough.

We know *The Miami Vice Scrapbook* will satisfy some of those appetites.

MIAMI VICE

One hour before *Miami Vice*'s second season premiere, the TV critic on the most serious news show of all, *The McNeil/Lehrer News Hour*, stood in front of a camera and proceeded to knock the hell out of a cops and robbers show, a TV show so radically different it was nominated for a record breaking 15 Emmy Awards, including best dramatic series, best actor in a dramatic series and best supporting actor in a dramatic series (which it won).

What did the critic have to say? "The 15 Emmy Award nominations say more about bad TV than they do about good TV. *Miami Vice* is just bad MTV (Music Television)."

The critic continued, "Viewers have been snookered by the look. Under the glitz, it isn't very good. These are cops who wear sharp clothes, they dress like criminals, which is improbable. Real life cops don't look chic. Where are they supposed to get the money to live like this?"

The very intellectual critic then continued to pan the dialogue, the music, the scenery and the actors, misidentifying their Ferrari as a souped-up Corvette, describing Sonny Crockett (played by Don Johnson) and Ricardo [Rico] Tubbs [who calls himself "Tough, unique, bad, bold and sassy"] (played by Philip Michael Thomas) as "empty headed bimbos, clothes horses with nothing to say, beautiful, but dumb."

That same night, millions of eagerly anticipating viewers were tuned into the Fall '85 premiere of *Miami Vice*, a two hour tour-de-force (for a TV series) called "Prodigal Son." Directed by Paul Michael Glaser (Starsky in *Starsky and Hutch*), the opening scenes show Crockett and Tubbs, the impeccably dressed undercover vice cops from Miami, tromping around the Colombian jungles (actually Bear Mountain State Park on the New York/New Jersey border) to find an informant who will tell them how cocaine from South America gets to the Florida Everglades.

Strapped to a chair, with a dead chicken hanging over his head, and attached to an electric generator, the informant is being horribly tortured by official Latin American soldiers, who beat on Crockett and Tubbs when they try to stop it. They're told that this is the Latino way and that they are naive Americanos.

Bear Mountain Park, in New York State, was used to shoot a scene which was supposed to take place in the Columbian jungle.

Cut to Miami, where stone-faced Lt. Castillo (played by Emmy winner Edward James Olmos) decides that they'll stake out the swamps to stop a delivery. Two minutes later, after an intense gun battle, one hydrofoil, one airplane and all the bad guys are blown away.

The Colombians are crazos who take everything personally and therefore kill three cops in an Art Deco Miami hotel room in retaliation for the swamp bust. Seriously injuring Gina (Saundra Santiago), one of the regular troopers, Sonny and Rico convince Castillo they have to go to New York and get the bad guys. (When wounded Gina said she was cold, Sonny took his pristine Versace jacket and covered her, even though blankets were readily accessible.)

Cut to New York City, where Crockett and Tubbs immediately run into tough New York City cops who don't want to babysit. Within seconds, via one phone call and a jab in an uncooperative suspect's solar plexus, they prove they can take care of themselves and hit the streets of the city. What they can't understand is the NYPD's lack of cooperation.

Rico uses every public phone on the set in an attempt to locate Valerie Gordon (Pam Greer), a good looking New York cop who three weeks earlier was seen in a rerun, "Rites of Passage," blowing away her sister's murderer. (Obviously, she must have gotten

off easily, thanks to Sonny and Rico). In this episode, she, too, is undercover, and connected to one of the principal criminals in the case, who is shot by Rico, her long time lover.

Not to be outdone, it takes Sonny only a few minutes to get picked up by a beautiful blonde with an attitude problem. Thirty seconds later, he and she are doing mouth-to-mouth resuscitaton in the door of a New York City cab, as the driver grumbles about time on the meter.

Since the boys from Miami don't listen to reason, get no help from NYPD, and are generally harassed in the carrying out of their duties, Rico smells money and power gone sour.

Sonny's beautiful blonde turns out to be an informant for a high-priced banker's cartel concerned about their Latin American investments, so if Colombia wants to settle their foreign debt with cocaine sales, it's o.k. by them. However, it's not o.k. for Sonny and Rico to go around trying to stop the Colombian connection.

Sonny's lover immediately sees the error of her ways ("I'm not supposed to fall in love with the mark.") and tells them who's behind the hit team.

First, Sonny and Rico cut off the Colombians' supply by finding the drop and blowing a storefront away.

Then we witness the killing of three hit men responsible for the murder of the duo's "connection" in a marvelously decorated Soho loft.

Before the story was resolved, Sonny and Rico got through some very steamy scenes with their girl friends. Both men know how to kiss and aren't afraid to prove it. Passing that point, the suggestive bedroom scenes were positively erotic. Truly sensuous. Sexy. Hot.

The boys get to knock off some more of the competition and blow up a helicopter after a shoot out at Lincoln Center. No Chagall windows were broken. Amazing. More amazing was that they always found parking in the city.

Through it all, one is constantly aware of the trademarks that have made *Miami Vice* so popular: the high fashion outfits, the fast cars (black Ferrari convertible in Miami, yellow Cadillac, circa 1969, in New York) and the music, hot and sizzling...or cool and laid back, depending on which seamy side of the rich life was being shown.

Never did New York look more like Miami. The truth is, though, that New York has its own treasure trove of Art Deco architecture, which Executive Producer Michael Mann took full advantage of. Some of the skyscraper scenes were shot as if the cameraman were lying on the sidewalk, with dizzying towers swirling overhead. It's the way one imagines New York looks to a first time tourist.

"In New York we were as selective about what we shot and as expressionistic in our depiction as in Miami. We showed the city, but we showed it our way," said Mann.

John Nicolella, who's in charge of the budget and actual production (he looks like Luciano Pavarotti, the chubby, bearded opera star), admitted, "This is the most different approach to New York that I've ever seen and I've worked on such films set in Manhattan as Woody Allen's *Interiors* and *Saturday Night Fever.*

"Every production company that comes into town has the same menu: The Plaza Hotel, the Empire State Building, Central Park, Times Square, the Statue of Liberty. We didn't shoot any of those sights (they pan the Chrysler Building, though, and it never looked better). We've taken a delicate approach to a really tough town.

"It takes a lot of nerve to get out there and give up Times Square. We're doing *Miami Vice* and that look exists in New York. We found buildings on Wall Street that take your breath away, skyscrapers with arched windows, a conference room in which a 1930's elevator

comes out of the floor." (It sure does, corpse and all!)

A downtown street was chosen as a backdrop for a chase scene because it contained a basic black wrought iron building, a purple building with soft green hues and a paisley building. But there's so much action, so much going on between the characters, you barely have time to notice the details, even though you KNOW they're there.

The *McNeil/Lehrer* critic had no idea what he was missing. Except for the commercial breaks, which seemed interminable compared to the show, the two hours flew by, jammed with action, violence, eroticism, camaraderie, and character development. *Miami Vice* is great TV, not unlike a feature film. Definitely better than some of the rejects desperate cable TV watchers are fed.

Miami Vice is different TV. Different even from *Hill Street Blues*, the acclaimed cop show, also on NBC, which led to *Miami Vice*'s development.

Brandon Tartikoff was wondering how to work some kind of music video format into NBC's programming in

Chatting on a New York City street corner as they prepare to film a scene.

Sonny and Rico sound and look like the parts they have to play.

a way to best benefit the network. One of his scribbled notes read, "MTV cops." Anthony Yerkovich, then working as a producer and writer for *Hill Street* was asked to write a script for a pilot. At that time (which is when Philip Michael Thomas first heard about it), it was still called *Gold Coast*.

Recalls Yerkovich, "Even when I was on *Hill Street Blues* I was collecting information about Miami. I thought of it as a sort of modern day American Casablanca. It seemed to be an interesting socio-economic tidepool: the incredible number of refugees from Central America and Cuba, the already extensive Cuban-American community. And on top of all that, the drug trade. There's a fascinating amount of service industries that revolve around the drug trade—money laundering, bail bondsmen, attorneys who service drug smugglers. Miami has become a sort of Barbary Coast enterprise gone beserk."

It is that kind of fertile soil which brings forth our heroes, Sonny Crockett and Ricardo Tubbs, who engage in a fierce battle for truth, justice and the American Way. (Philip Michael Thomas especially likes *Superman III* and *Mighty Mouse*.) The bad guys are BAD, and the good guys have to decide whether they'll walk the line or fall into the temptations of the evil which surrounds them.

Miami Vice is Black hats vs. White hats, The Lone Ranger and Tonto, *The Untouchables* and *Superman* rolled into one show, packed with music, music and music.

Every Friday night, Crocket and Tubbs descend into the underworld, dressed in mufti, to fight our battles for us. The netherworld is high on drugs, power and money. Sonny and Rico sound and look like the parts they have to play, and can be tempted very easily. Often, as in the New York episode, payoffs are dangled in front of them. (Attention critics: How successful can an undercover cop be if he sticks out like a sore thumb? How can they afford the lifestyle? Expense account.)

Sometimes the straight cops worry about other cops who cross the line to the other side.

The pilot, which ran in 1984, dealt with these themes in a now familiar way. Sonny Crockett was marked for death by Calderone, a Colombian drug dealer responsible for his partner's death. Calderone hires an efficient Argentinian hit man to do the job. Enter Rico Tubbs, who's taken a leave of absence from NYPD to go after this same guy, who's responsible for killing Rico's older brother, also a cop, during a botched bust. During Rico's flashbacks of his brother's murder, Jan Hammer wrote and overlaid a haunting melody played on a South American flute.

Sonny and Rico reluctantly agree to work together, but when their connection to Calderone is blown away by the Argentinian, Sonny suspects that a police officer was acting as an informant. In the meantime, he and Rico get to Bimini, where Calderone is hiding out, and Rico falls in love with Calderone's daughter, Angelina, getting things even more complicated than they already were, but definitely heating up the screen. The flute, heard during the flashbacks, was repeated rythmically through what *Rolling Stone* called "an uncommonly sensuous love scene."

The informant turned out to be Sonny Crockett's ex-partner.

Thomas Carter, who did the work on the pilot, was encouraged to find creative ways to use music.

"What I felt was happening to Crockett at one point was that he had lost touch with reality. His marriage had fallen apart, and his ex-partner was leaking information to the bad guys. What I wanted to do was not to use the music as just background, but as psychological subtext. So I said, 'I want to do a sequence with Crockett and Tubbs in a car, lay some music over it, and I think they should drive somewhere.' I came up with the idea of using a Phil Collins tune, 'In The Air Tonight.' That is probably the prototypical *Miami Vice* sequence," he concludes.

Are these story lines and techniques enough to carry the show? Some people say no. They claim that pretty photography and good music make violence look good and that the music and visual impact of the show have taken away from character development and coherent dialogue.

Lee Katzin, who directed an episode called "Cool Runnin'," admits that "the show is written for an MTV audience, which is more interested in images, emotions and energy than plot and character and words."

Why is the music so important and is it really an MTV ripoff?

"I've been asked if we were doing the same thing as MTV," remarks the driven 40-year-old who is the key to *Miami Vice*'s success, Michael Mann, executive producer, chain smoker, adventurer. "We're not. If the whole video approach—stylized film along to song—is considered a movement, which it is, then you could say we're first cousins."

The idea of putting film to music was first done in the 1930s by Sergei Eisenstein, the revolutionary film maker. "We haven't invented the Hula Hoop. If anything, we're only contemporary. And if we're different from the rest of TV, it's because the rest of TV isn't even contemporary."

There's no stale music in *Miami Vice* (they won an Emmy for music). Fred Lyle, the music coordinator, gets to pick the best of the top 40s charts for each show and to work with Jan Hammer, the musical genius who wrote the *Miami Vice* theme song (a hit single from the album) and does all the scoring. *Miami Vice* doesn't believe in remakes, either. They pay for original songs.

Which means you get to hear The Pointer Sisters, Tina Turner, Phil Collins, Billy Ocean, U2, Todd Rundgren, Frankie Goes to Hollywood, and even the Coasters doing "Poison Ivy," a '50s rock and roll classic.

How do the episodes come into being? Mann, the maniacal dictator who commands loyalty from his troops, tells a story:

"I got stopped for speeding on Collins Avenue. The cop says, 'Where are you going?' I say, 'The production office of *Miami Vice*. He says, 'Oh, you work on *Miami Vice*? I say, 'Yeah, I'm the executive producer.' He says, 'Oh, I got a great story for you.' He forgets all about writing me a ticket, he gives me a great story and I use it. This show is a ball. It's absolutely a blast.

Miami Vice *is black hats vs. white hats.*

"I mean, how else do you get to tell 22 stories a year? Or hear a song like 'Smuggler's Blues' on the radio and say, 'Wow! Those lyrics are fantastic. Let's do an episode on it.' Think, who knows this—better than anybody? Mikey—you know Miguel Pinero (author of Short Eyes and an ex-con). Get him to write a script, have lunch with Glenn Frey (formerly of The Eagles and writer/singer of "Smuggler's Blues") two days later and ask him if he wants to play Jimmy, the pilot. Bang, it's on the air in four weeks."

This time, Sonny and Rico reluctantly pose as cocaine importers in Colombia to find out who has been ripping off drug smugglers. It's a hair raising assignment that has local police, bandits and assorted pistoleros all gunning for them, and it's their job to set a trap for a vicious kidnapper.

Jimmy, a "spaced-out pilot who left part of his cerebral cortex in Viet-Nam," agrees to fly them to South America and back. And while he professes no allegiance, they rely on him for emergency relief if they make their Colombian connection, knowing that if they ever make it back to Miami, the fun and games would really start.

In the climactic scene, Trudy (Olivia Brown), a fellow officer used as bait, is wired to blow up by the bad guy, another cop gone bad. A federal agent remarks, "I can smell 'em, but I can't understand 'em," as Frey's lyrics rise over the scene and the camera pans away to reveal Crockett and Tubbs comforting a forgotten Trudy.

Frank Lyle did the music overlays for Mann, who wanted to create tension between the music and the action. (The episode was yet another one directed by Paul Michael Glaser.) "Instead of doing the whole show and letting Frey's song tell the pain and anguish of being a smuggler at the end, over the credits, like you'd expect on TV, we're using the song maybe eight times throughout the show. You're in a scene, and all of a sudden, up comes Frey singing, 'It's the lure of easy money. It's got very strong appeal.' And you fade out again. It's like a Greek chorus, coming to chant 'Fear him. Fear him.'"

The song is part of the *Miami Vice* album that was released by MCA in September '85 and quickly climbed the charts. The record contains the flute music from "Calderone's Demise" and other themes written by Jan Hammer, with cuts by Chaka Khan, Tina Turner and Phil Collins.

Every 10 days or so, a cassette of the unfinished episode is flown by courier to a farmhouse near Brewster, N.Y., where the Czech born composer adds the

Glenn Frey (Center) with Don Johnson and Philip Michael Thomas.

moody musical scores that credit him with two Emmy nominations. Working in a state-of-the-art studio with a Moog synthesizer, a Fairlight CMI (a digital player and recorder) a guitar, a piano, and anything else he needs, Hammer hurriedly lays in the musical tracks that have drawn critical raves for integration with the action.

Says Hammer: "The old style was for the composer to sit in production meetings and someone would say, 'Let's put something here, let's put something there.' We have managed to by-pass all that. The only time I talk with Michael (Mann) is when he wants even more music.

"Once I finished a show two days before airdate. I may get it ten days or so before it airs, but I keep getting constant revisions in the story content. I cannot get serious about the music until about four or five days before it airs. It's a real high pressured job."

Jan's name is synonymous with the progressive fusion of rock and jazz from the early 1970s. Though he scored feature films, he had no intention of working in TV until Michael Mann got in touch with him through a mutual friend.

"We had an informal meeting before the pilot was filmed. He was looking for something unconventional, and he was concerned about the look and sound of the new series. It was the first time I had been asked to do a TV series. My gut reaction was, 'This is a cop show. It might be nice, but so what? *Magnum P.I.* in Miami.' But I knew Mann was an adventurer. I read the script and I knew it was good, too. I wrote something. He liked it, and we were on our way."

Aside from the pressure of an unforgiving deadline, Hammer has complete freedom to compose whatever fits the scenes. "The limitations are all within me. That's what's so wonderful about this arrangement."

Since the success of *Miami Vice*, he has been inundated with offers and invitations to score other series and feature films, in addition to pursuing his separate recording career.

"I need no pressure during production breaks. I need some time to recharge my batteries. I had to give up some big offers, TV series, left and right, and a Dick Clark movie. But I love *Miami Vice* so much, I've already agreed to do another year. My manager has standing instructions to say no to other offers. I don't even want to know what they are."

In the meantime, Hammer continues to play beat-the-clock. "I like the show...it's exciting, attractive, has sex appeal, mystique—and great music. It gives you your MTV fix."

The show is certainly attractive, and even the detractors admit it. Producer John Nicolella in Miami says, "Michael is in charge of the whole visual sense of the show...all this slick stuff. Which car, what the clothes look like, the colors, the kind of film cutting. He says, 'It will be this and this and this,' and he maintains it all along. He also found a nut like me who will follow it to the end of the world."

Bobby Roth directed one episode (now he's the executive producer of one of the *Miami Vice* rip-offs) and has this to say: "There is a very definite attempt to give the show a particular look. There are certain colors you are not allowed to shoot. Such as red and brown. If the script says 'A Mercedes pulls up here,' the car people will show you three or four different Mercedes. One will be white, one will be black, one will be silver. You will not get a red one or a brown one.

"Michael knows how things are going to look on camera. A lot of its is very basic stuff that has never been applied to TV. For example, Michael carried a water truck around with him on his movie *Thief*, watering the streets down. So I decided to water the streets at night in my episode of *Miami Vice*. You get a different look, a beautiful reflection of moonlight off the pavement.

"I found this house that was really perfect," continues Roth, "but the color was sort of beige. The art department instantly painted the house gray for me. Even on feature films people try to deliver what is necessary, but not more. At *Miami Vice* they start with what's necessary and go beyond it."

The same is true of the wardrobe department.

"The concept of the show is to be on top of all the latest fashion trends in Europe," says Bambi Breakstone, the costume designer. Sonny and Rico wear five to eight outfits per episode, always in approved colors: pink, blue, green, fuschia...and the like.

Don Johnson says, "The viewers may see me in an outfit for only five or ten minutes, but I sometimes have to wear it for days or weeks. By the time the show is over, it's dead to me, even though the actual fashions haven't hit the streets. In fact, I wore a variation of my *Miami Vice* clothing before I did the show. I figured a T-shirt, jeans and a sport coat were right for anything short of meeting the Queen."

Philip Michael Thomas says the only way he gets to keep his wardrobe is if he buys it. "You don't get anything from *Miami Vice* that you don't earn."

Pam Grier and Phillip Michael Thomas in the "Rites of Passage" episode of Miami Vice.

You can bet there are plenty of people in the fashion industry cashing in on the *Miami Vice* pacesetters.

"The show has taken Italian men's fashion and spread it to mass America," claims an executive at Bloomingdale's. "Sales of unconstructed blazers, fabric jackets and lighter colors have gone up noticeably." Kenneth Cole is doing a shoe line named for "Crockett" and "Tubbs," After Six is doing evening wear and Macy's opened a *Miami Vice* department in men's and boys' wear departments.

Add all these elements together and then wonder if the violence that is so much a part of the show is indeed too pretty for the critics.

Miami civic fathers were concerned about the city's slimy underbelly as it's exposed in the show. Now, with revenues from the show at over $1,000,000 per episode, they don't cry as much. In fact, Don Johnson and Philip Michael Thomas have received the keys to the city. Dade County police, who appreciate the show's realism, consult on the show, and have offered storylines to the crew.

Network censors, the people from Broadcast Standards, have cut scenes they have considered too graphic. Says producer Nicolella, "I choose not to judge the impact of violence in our show. I don't believe the show is capable of inflicting as much damage as parents can at home."

Mike Levine, an NBC executive, claims that shows with cartoon violence, where shotguns go off and no one gets hurt, might be even more insidious than the realistic violence on *Miami Vice*. "*Miami Vice* pushes the Broadcast Standards people as far up against the wall as it can, in an attempt to be realistic. They go for it all, and Standards will pull them back."

Never one to approve censorship, Don Johnson describes a scene in which he had to shoot to kill. He doesn't feel the violence is gratuitous, it simply reflects the day to day realities of life-threatening police work. "There was one scene we did that caused more uproar and got more mail, pro and con, because we pulled the trigger. It was in an episode where we shot from the hip.

"We were up against the wall, making up scenes as we were going along. Michael Mann wrote the scene and gave it to me over the phone. I was trying to rescue a little girl being held hostage by this guy. Michael told me, 'This is what happens. The guy says, "If I twitch, she's gone." Your line is, "Maybe you won't even twitch." Then you blow him away.' I wanted to suspend time, and the way I read the line was what made it sell. I went "Maybe...you won't even ...twitch." BOOM! The cadence threw him—and the audience—off. It was devastating.

"But then the violence in our show is not cartoon violence: it's real—which I think is a deterrent, and not an encouragement. When someone goes down, he bleeds and stays down. And because we use a process called step-printing, in which you print the same frame twice, it appears as staccato slow motion, which heightens the reality and the violent tone.

"I'm immersed in the character and weighing rights and wrongs—legally and morally—of what I'm about to do when I pull the trigger. Well, morality is not a question that Crockett answers. It's what he does."

"Take a chance, take a chance," Nicolella exhorts the crew. "The attrition rate here is incredible," says Michael Mann. "It's like a race car—say you're driving at Daytona. You have to go 500 miles. You've driven the race car right, if after the 500th mile, it cannot do the 501st. You've used everything up."

Anthony Yerkovich, creator of *Miami Vice* concedes. "In the long run, you can rely only so much on color coding and Bauhaus architecture and the Versace spring catalogue. As soon as they get a handle on the scripts, the show will burn rubber."

Bobby Roth concludes, "The old stigma against TV is gone now. A lot of shows are going to sound better and they are going to look better. And I think *Miami Vice* is a big reason for that."

Yes, indeed.

(*Overleaf*) "Miami Vice *pushes the Broadcast Standards people as far up against the wall as it can, in an attempt to be realistic.*"

PHILIP MICHAEL THOMAS

"He turned, looked directly into my eyes, and said, 'Hi.' I mumbled something. I couldn't focus on anything but his hypnotic hazel eyes. And there, before my stare, they changed colors. After forever, I watched his voluptuous mouth as he talked to me. I couldn't hear a thing he said. Those pearly white teeth. Those lips. My God. Falling hopelessly for this man could be so, so easy!"

That's how one lady friend describes her first meeting with Philip Michael Thomas, the minister (ordained at 15) and former theology student (Oakwood College in Huntsville, Alabama and UCLA/Berkeley, where he drove his philosophy teachers crazy), who plays Ricardo Tubbs opposite Don Johnson's Sonny Crockett in Miami Vice.

Even press professionals are not immune to his animal magnetism. Wrote one: "He sits facing me on the sofa. He has high Indian cheekbones, long lashes, green eyes and suggestions of colors from alizarian to topaz in his tawny skin. He seems comfortable with his good looks and radiates great energy and warmth. His steady eye contact exerts an almost physical pull. He listens carefully, his words are sung, machine gunned, preached, Jamaican accented, rapped."

"Everything that's happened to me is a continuation of leaps and bounds towards success. (He started in show business at the age of four, playing roles in feature films, with his mother's guidance.) It's not the destination, but the journey that matters most."

He decided on his game plan, code-named E.G.O.T. (Emmy, Grammy, Oscar and Tony, all of which he intends to win or be nominated for), after he saw an excellent West Coast production of *Hair* with Ben Vereen. As a young seminarian, he auditioned and played Hud in the San Francisco version of the same play. He was already nominated for an Emmy in 1979 for *Angel Dust: The Whack Attack*, and played roles in many, many TV series, like *Starsky and Hutch*.

"I've just climbed Mt. Olympus. Steven Spielberg calls and wants me to be in his next movie. I get calls from Nancy Reagan. The Queen of England wants me to go over. I've become greened, like money. I respect the position. I'm enthusiastic, God-inspired. I don't think I'm a big s--t, though, because the higher I climb

"I've been a ladies' man since my school days."

on the ladder of success, the humbler I get. I know you're only as good as your last two minutes and 45 seconds. I don't run from people who want autographs. I stay and sign and take that energy back with me and am creative. I'm smart enough to know that as long as the people have something to believe in, the gods will exist."

"I respond to my environment and what is going on. In that way, an actor is like an undercover cop. I plug into what's around me. I'm always open and respectful. If you close the door, it might not be open tomorrow. Yesterday's a cancelled check, tomorrow's a promissory note, and today is cash in hand. I see every day as a step."

He has starred in 11 motion pictures, including *Black Fist, The Book of Numbers, Sparkle,* and *Stigma,* all of which he wants to release in a Philip Michael Thomas Film Festival. He also plans to set up an arts foundation for the needy.

"I have lived my life through my religious studies. I don't try to preach to people. I'm not interested in saving anyone's soul because God can do that. I would like to be an example to people, though."

Because of his deep religious convictions, Philip was apprehensive about doing a TV series since he is concerned about content and quality in productions involving him. But when he was offered *Miami Vice,* it was the first time he wanted to be involved, explaining that the producers spare no expense in turning out quality.

"I thank God for the part I play. To be one of the focal points of such a popular show is an incredible experience."

Philip's sexual dynamism wasn't created with *Miami Vice.* He was a ladies' man opposite Irene Cara in *Sparkle* and Freda Payne in *Book of Numbers.*

"I've been a ladies' man since my school days, chasing and being chased. Now I could take advantage of thousands of women, if I was just a flesh peddler. But I don't think in those terms. I'm much more interested in a relationship than a one-night stand. I don't like uninteresting anything. I like a woman to give me a run for my money. As for being pure, I like someone who looks good, smells good, tastes good.

Philip's sexual dynamism didn't begin with Miami Vice.

Philip Michael Thomas in the Warner Bros. film Sparkle.

"I've been called a sucker for trusting people easily, but I love people. If I love you, I will do anything, within reason. I'm not one to put chains on and ask questions. I love a woman who feels that way, too."

His schedule, and Don's, too, are full of things like being Grand Marshal in boating events and parades, Christmas benefits, Bar Mitzvahs, visits (signing autographs) to department stores, and fundraisers for organizations like the Black Opera Guild. There's no doubt about it. The man is in demand.

He's a chocolate cop. Not, of course, because he is naturally cafe au lait with green eyes. Not because he's the black undercover cop in *Miami Vice*. It's because he was out there trying to do some good in the world.

He recalls the raunchy fundraiser at Miami's Fountainbleu Hilton:

"We (he and Don Johnson) started out wearing robes, trunks, T-shirts and shoes. By the time we were through, and after the crowds of women implored "take it off, take it all off..." we were bombarded. (Don has four live-in bodyguards!) They were trying to touch us. It was like *Caligula*. Every race and creed. It was fantastic to be dipped in chocolate and have it kissed from my body.

"We took turns on a spring loaded seat over a 400 gallon vat of chocolate syrup, while the ladies paid $3 per pop. After every three splashdowns, they licked the chocolate off my hairy chest. The chocolate felt kind of good, actually. It was like a warm oil that you put all over your body. What was even more interesting was to see the hungry look in all the women's eyes. I had so many women come up to me."

Ah, well... chocolate will never be the same.

"Woman offer me gifts and trips to Paris. They've schemed and plotted just to get to meet me. Hundreds and hundreds of women have come to see me on the set for autographs and things like that. I love to flirt."

Being a sex symbol can have its downside, though. Because he's so good-looking, some people think he's all glitzy surface, shallow and empty. "Sometimes people say, 'I had no idea you could act. I thought you were just a pretty boy.'

"The other day I talked about these things, and I realized that I'm tired of people wanting to ---- me. It makes me ask when do d---s and p-----s become god and goddesses. Love is a completion, 360 degrees, not the exploitation of organs. You know what its like to get hit on and someone wants to jump your bones? Well, what if that person has AIDS or something? Someone thinks you look delicious and may try to give you a yard of tongue...they might have herpes. You have to be careful these days because there's a lot of illicit sex going on.

"There's a real difference between sharing love and ----ing. We live in a society that has all this soap opera love where people fall in love, but what they do is ----. They don't think anything of the person's well-being, what their goals are. All they want to do is get into their private parts."

How does he get around female entrapment without hurting the ladies' feelings?

"I manage. I flirt. I love to flirt. Then I zing them. 'How do you know you can handle me? How do you know I don't beat women?' The reaction varies. Sometimes they go along with it. If they stay with me for any length of time and continue to be aggresive, they always say, 'Wow. You're different than I thought you

E.G.O.T. (Emmy, Grammy, Oscar and Tony.)

were.'

"Being interested in someone's appearance is an outward expression of an inward submission to an idea. In my family there are very beautiful people. We've never been conceited in the sense of thinking that our physicality is so important.

"People always ask me what if feels like to be a sex symbol, but the way I look at it, I'm a health symbol because I'm a healthy man. That's why I'm almost 40 and can pass for 22. I'm not conceited. People tell me I'm so fine and handsome, but I think my internal self is much nicer than my external self. There's more to Philip Michael Thomas than meets the eye. It's not the clothes or the looks that make a person, it's the heart.

"That's why I came up with the concept of teaching people to care for themselves and their god-selves....If you're going to have a sexual encounter, prepare for it. Bathe in oils so you can be kissed anywhere and everywhere, to enjoy the nectar of the gods. It becomes more romantic, courting. Much more than, 'Hey baby, I see you, you see me. Let's get it on.' At some point I intended to put together a book dealing with the sensual delights according to my philosophy. I've already published a book of aphorisms."

Those who don't come in physical contact with him lust after him in letters. Some of them are steamy hot, others are raunchy and contain certain kinds of photos. Some of his mail is weird and XXX rated.

"I get thousands of letters. They come from all over—London, Australia. Most are very intelligent. I also get requests from chicks in the Army for posters of me with my chest showing. Fat girls write, 'I've lost 30 pounds and I'm preparing for you. You're the handsomest man I've ever seen on earth. During your love scenes, I'm having sex with my husband, but I'm thinking of you.' I take it all with a grain of salt, because even if I were the most sexual man in the world, there's no way I could take on all the women who want me."

Philip is, after all, the theology student who became a TV knight in shining armor. He's more laid back, but he's out there on the *Miami Vice* set with Don Johnson, pushing limits to the max. His exuberance and energy are in contrast to Johnson's drive, perfection and moodiness. "I replenish myself by giving, and it comes back," he declares.

How does Philip feel about the relationship between the two of them on and off the screen?

"We trained with each other. I told Don about E.G.O.T., and he told me about some dreams he

wanted to develop. So we made an effort to work out together, to jog together before the sun rose, to learn our lines together. We trained with policemen in undercover work. Don knows a lot more about guns than I do, so he taught me about weapons. During the making of the pilot, we practically lived with each other. We worked on Saturdays and Sundays, and you don't get paid for those days. And we always gave each other space, because we didn't want to force a relationship. We just wanted to be together so we could find out how we functioned. There isn't time now. We work 12-18 hours a day, five days a week, so when we do go home, we sleep."

Don explains that their first on-screen relationship has become a model for adult male bonding in the '80s. "There's a boredom with traditional male relationships—no touching, no holding, no genuine closeness, none of that stuff that might be misconstrued. And that's the way most actors have portrayed them, out of fear." Philip says it's true. People come up to him and tell him he's a guy, not a cop. They've also named their pets after the characters.

How does Philip feel about his role as Ricardo Tubbs, the spark of the show, the counterpoint to Sonny Crockett's bravado?

"I'm out there, fighting for things, going for things. Don's ego is out there. He wants to be the Great White Hope and I say fine. I can deal with that. Our tension forms a connection that makes people whisper, 'What's that? What are they doing?' You know... 'Who's going to explode next?' Besides, Don's ego may be serious, but there's a part of him that's very spiritual, that is, you know, like a pussycat. Don is real intense on the set. He maps out the way he wants to go. I just do it.

"My success in the role led to an offer to do a national commercial. It tripped me out. For years, since 1972, I went to all the agencies and they would look at me and say, 'What are you?' 'I'm an American, a man.' They'd come back at me: 'What is your parentage?' they couldn't categorize me, and everywhere I went they told me I couldn't be hired because I'm too exotic looking. But when people put you in a category and say you can't do this, you can't do that, and you know you have the ability to do it, it's frustrating. Now they say I'm doing a national commercial, and I say, 'Bring it on, Baby!'"

Philip describes himself as "American Gumbo," part Irish, American Indian, German and Black.

"I don't like limitations, no matter what I'm doing. I never limited anyone in my life, and I don't like being

"During the making of the pilot, we pratically lived with each other. We worked on Saturdays and Sundays, and you don't get paid for those days."

limited. When people categorize you, they're telling you, you can't do this, you can't do that. You have the ability to do it, but they won't allow you to. It amazes me that now that I'm part of a hit TV series, a multi-million dollar one, which became #1, all the doors that were closed to me before are opening. I think it's fantastic that I've been able to retain my integrity. I haven't messed over anybody or done anything I regret in the process of building my career. What is taking place is they are coming after me because of the quality of the work I'm doing in the industry. And frankly, I like that.

"Did you see the show with Calderone's demise? I fell in love with his daughter? It was a sizzling affair. Did you see The Great McCarthy where I had the love affair with the lady that killed the black woman? That one sparked some things across the nation that made people take notice and say, 'Whoah...what's going on here?' I'm in a rare position because they never let black men kiss and make love on TV.

"Roger E. Moseley sent me a telegram signed, 'from one of your favorite friends.' Michael Warren from *Hill Street Blues* was talking to my brother the other day and he applauded me. 'Hey, man,' he said, 'You're the first.' I'm the only black man in the United States starring in a major dramatic series. It's a heavy space to be in, and I really do intend to walk away with the image."

In "Rites of Passage," he offers to help an old flame (Pam Greer, who plays a New York City cop) locate her missing younger sister, who doesn't want to abandon life in the express lane. They find her hooked on cocaine and the property of a smooth call girl operator, who has her murdered when she changes her mind.

During the investigation, Rico gets it on with the lady from New York, and it was visually and sensually satisfying. Steam was coming out of the speakers on the TV set. At the end of the episode, it looked as if

Jane Pauley, co-host of NBC's Today Show, *interviews Philip Michael Thomas as he takes a break between filming scenes from* Miami Vice.

Posing for the camera on the rooftop of the Puck Building in New York City.

Pam was going to be put away forever, but in the premiere of the Fall '85 season, which was shot in New York City, she was back (as an undercover vice cop) and so were the steamy scenes.

How did he get the role of Ricardo Tubbs in the first place?

"It was just like when Shadrach, Mischach and Abednego came out of the fiery furnace and the only things singed were the shackles that were placed on their hands. they had their health, their strength...everything. And they shouted with joy. It's a joy, a great experience.

"They auditioned about 300 people. When I came in to read for the network, the fire that happened between Don Johnson and me was magic. It was like an explosive compulsion of a new affection. And everyone knew the combination of the two of us was the magic that they needed to make partners work on TV. They were looking for a team, and I brought fire and Don brought equal fire. The rest is history.

"I had a sixth sense about it. I first heard about it in October of '83. It was *Gold Coast* then, and I read the initial script. the character reminded me of a Jamaican character I played in *Starsky and Hutch*. When I met Tony Yerkovich, he said that it fit his conception of the wild, flamboyant type represented by Texas St. Jock. I told him he didn't need to look any further. I sealed it in my mind at the initial meeting.

"My grandfather told me, years ago, that all I see belongs to me. And it eventually did. There was land in the family for hundreds of years and I claimed it. Just like I claimed the part. But then I got a call from my agent and he said that they wouldn't be able to use me. I found out later they screen tested different people. I thought to myself that I wouldn't let that happen to me. Before I knew it, I got the call, along with some 20 other guys to come read for the network. There were 10 Crocketts and 10 Tubbs. I read with three or four

Signing autographs for many of the media people who attended a Miami Vice *press conference at the Visage nightclub in New York City.*

Arriving at the 37th Annual Emmy Awards in Pasadena, Cal.

other guys, before I read with Don, and it was o.k., but it wasn't THE connection.

"I was walking out the door and into the elevator, when Milt Hamerman, NBC's VP for talent, came out and asked me if I would read one more time. When I walked in the door I saw Don. I didn't know a thing about his career and he didn't know anything about mine. We didn't even bother going out to read it when they asked us to. It was a cold reading. This was it. I'm telling you the fire... we just tore it up. It just hit. Kajung. Afterwards there was no question in my mind that we were the ones to be chosen. He's a Sagittarian and I'm a Gemini. Exact opposites—fire and air. We had instant chemistry.

"Now I'm constantly happy, but I don't get excited the way I used to. I don't call up and make cheerleader noises anymore. Excitement is shortlived and leads to disappointment. Now I'm enthusiastic, which mean God intoxicated. My internal juices are continuing to develop and create an awareness in me that this is right, that I'm producing at the peak of my quality. I've claimed it, because I earned it. I accepted what was mine."

What is it like for Philip to be a hot shot star?

"Your time is not your own. I mean, really. All I know is that the driver picks me up and takes me to work. The makeup man comes in, the wardrobe man comes in, they make sure everything is together. My breakfast is there, we read our lines and set the scene and go to work. It's a grueling experience.

"It's fine that I can practice my art. The financial rewards are great. The public rewards are great. But I do miss a personal life, there is no personal life, and I do get tired. Sunday is really the only day I have off. I'm working six and seven days a week because on the weekends, we usually have events that take place.

"It's more a physical exhaustion (they can shoot for 12-18 hours a day, in season) than a mental or spiritual thing. Like when I and Don were both sick. But if I had my way, I wouldn't sleep. Getting by on the two to four hours I do now means no longer accepting the limitations that once bound me. Now I do the drug called life, which is so abundant. I'm just letting the light shine in.

Striking a mock shoot-em-up to cheering fans at the Emmys, Sept. '85.

Taking a break on location at Bear Mountain Park, New York.

"I have very little time to see friends. The best time to catch me is on the set, so I haven't been able to see personal friends. My brother, George, is here with me now, though, as my bodyguard. He's younger, 25, and I think he's handsomer than I am. When I look at him, he looks like God to me. He's about 6'4", 200 pounds of fat and muscle with green eyes. I'm keeping it in the family. They hired a bodyguard for me, and I said that if someone was going to guard my body, I want him to be close to me and close to my consciousness. So I sent for my brother, and he's enjoying it. I feel very well protected. I look at this big ol' tall dude and I remember when I used to smack him on the side of head. It's nice."

Even after the long hours and the strenuous shoots, he can be seen chatting with the local gawkers, posing for pictures, mugging for children and preparing for yet one more charity event.

Philip is meticulous about his health. The refrigerator in his dressing trailer is full of mango and peach nectars, fruit juice and mineral water. (Unlike the business atmosphere of partner Don's trailer, Philip's is done in raspberry, and there are clothes, books and papers strewn all over the place.)

"I thank my mother and father for creating me. I don't mind the sexual image, but that's not the one I project. I only go out of my way to be healthy. I might be 36, but I feel like I'm 25. And for that I thank God. I'm basically a vegetarian, but since I've come to Florida, I've eaten more meat than I have in 15 years, and I've gained weight. Weight shows on TV, but I'm basically thin. I range between 150-55, but I've been ranging between 160-170, which I'm carrying well. With all those benefit suppers I attend, I must eat to be polite.

"Since I've worked on my record album (released in June '85), I had to go back on the diet I was used to. I miss jogging my 5-13 miles a day, and I haven't been able to go out to the gym and workout. The physical intensity is necessary for me to stay peaked.

"I keep my skin clear because I wear very little make up. I just wear base. Basically, what you see is all me. People come up to me and see me for the first time 'in person.' They think I look better than I do on TV. TV doesn't do anything for you. I use different

A tense Detective Tubbs takes cover in "White Bread" on NBC-TV's Miami Vice.

Detectives Crockett and Tubbs are shocked to find their main connection to a dangerous drug kinpin has been assassinated.

mineral baths and maintain the taking of herbs. I do internal cleansing, which keeps me young and vibrant. It's basic to my success, and it's inside and out.

"I've used internal and external tecniques of cleanliness over the years. I don't have any vices (no pun intended), and I don't take drugs, not even aspirin."

Have the financial rewards of spectacular success led to splurging?

"I'm not a splurger. I do put my money into my music. Which is part 2 of the Master Plan. I incorporated my own company, PMT International in 1984. The name of the record company is 'Spaceship' because I love to fly, and now I've produced my own album, and there will be films, too. My splurging is my investment in myself. I spent $100,000."

With "E" for Emmy on its way, Philip is ambitiously and energetically pursing the rest of the E.G.O.T. Master Plan. "G" for Grammy may be possible in 1986.

According to a friend (female, of course) who previewed a tape of some of the cuts on the album before its release, the songs are fantastic and have hit written all over them. "It discloses, more than any story you read, how sensuous Philip is, revealing a very intimate side of him. His voice is totally seductive."

Says Philip, "I've already done a number, 'Undercover Lover' on the show and I got a good response to it. I did one song last February ('85) called 'All My Love.' My brother cut three tunes in Los Angeles, and I did another five. During Christmas break, I was in the studio working on the master, and it was released in June, 1985.

"I've co-produced and co-wrote most of the songs (partner and fellow musician Don Johnson was seen dashing off to the recording studio with him). The title of the album is *Living the Book of My Life*. I don't plan

tour, but I will have videos and would like to have a TV special with music on it. And I've sent a tape with lyrics to Irene Cara (with whom he co-starred in *Sparkle*), but I haven't heard from her yet.

"My music, I feel, is better than a lot of what's out here, because I've been able to work on it for a long time and I've had a lot of experience. I play all kinds of instruments, too. Just like Prince, for a while no one knew who he was, but he put an album together and Wow! I have this Gemini quality of being a jack of all trades and master of many."

Philip is also working on the Oscar for his role in a movie. He plans to re-release his old films, *Stigma* and *Sparkle*, and do a sequel called *Sparkle II*. At the end of the Fall '85 shooting season, he hopes to work on a film script that was written and given to him by Oscar Williams, who directed him in his Emmy nomination performance in *Angel Dust: The Whack Attack*. It's already on the boards for Cannon Films and Carl Reiner was also asked to meet with him about a role in a forthcoming motion picture.

Philip isn't neglecting the last part of E.G.O.T., either. He's going after the Tony Award with his musical play, *The Legend of Stagger Lee*. The play, based on the old Rock and Roll favorite, contains 22 songs, 12 of them written by you-know-who. Preliminary discussions with Ben Vereen, who would play Billy opposite Philip's Stagger Lee, have already taken place. The production is already being storyboarded for Broadway.

Philip also wants to buy the rights to the Pulitzer-prize winning play, *No Place to be Somebody*, in which he starred on Broadway, so that the Tony attack is taking place on two fronts.

How does he feel about everything falling into place so quickly?

"I think it's God. You can't stop a child whose time has come...I go down to the ocean here as much as possible, because that's where I find freedom and can be close to God. A lot of times in my life when I've dreamed about things and wanted to make them happen, there's a series of events that take place. Usually the idea would spark something within me. And I'll see it, visualize it, create the mental equivalent and then allow the seed to be planted in me, in the soil of my own mind. And then I will find myself around water. And when I go to the ocean, it's like a ritual, you know, to pray, I guess. It seems to bring a message and all of a sudden, because I'm listening, it makes me tranquil, it makes me feel good. Next thing you know, I'm into it, and I thank God for all of this."

And *Miami Vice*?

"This is a stepping stone for me to something far greater, and it's a great, great stepping stone."

DON JOHNSON

It was Darryl Zanuck who brought good guys vs. bad guys to the silver screen before TV was invented. He decided to plan his production policies around current events, and in 1930, it was the FBI against the gangsters. This became a brand new kind of entertainment which carried its tradition to the TV screen. In 1985, Miami is a center of crime in the U.S.A. and *Miami Vice* keeps its scripts close to reality, too.

In 1931, Spencer Tracy, the hero of *Quick Millions*, says that he is too nervous to steal and too lazy to work, but that a man is a fool to go into legitimate business when he can clean up in organized crime.

Don Johnson, the delectable undercover detective in *Miami Vice* (Sonny Crockett), didn't go into organized crime, but he did once admit that what kept him in the acting business was that he was "too lazy to work and too scared to steal."

When Don was visited by a reporter on the set of *Miami Vice*, it was 2:30 a.m. and cold. She walked into a very business-like trailer that was pin-neat. It was clear from her description that Don is totally involved in his work, living in almost Spartan elegance, obvi-

ously wanting things to be as perfect as possible. Co-star Philip Michael Thomas described him in a now-famous *Time* cover story as "The truck driver...real intense. He maps out the way he wants to go."

Recently accused in the media of having a swelled head and being an egomaniac, especially when it comes to production standards, even partner Thomas admits: "It's not a matter of Don's conceit. We have a responsibility of making the directors look good so they won't make us look bad."

When you find out how young Donnie Wayne started out in Flatt Creek, Missouri (the Show Me state), you can really see how close he is to realizing the dreams he had at 15 and 16 years old. Dreams do come true, but only if you work your way through the school of life, the school of hard knocks. Perhaps he's so convincing and sexy and vulnerable as Sonny Crockett because he started learning early.

In an old and dusty filing cabinet there was a folder full of clippings about the now very glamorous sexy star, which were very interesting and shed light on his style and personality.

The grandson of a preacher man.

Years ago, when Don got a starring role during the "Operation Prime Time" mini-series wars in *From Here to Eternity*, NBC released a summary of Don's life which gave the essentials in a really brief, way, labeled in capital letters and underlined:

BIOGRAPHICAL SUMMARY—DON JOHNSON

Birthplace: Flatt Creek, MO. (One old article in L.A.'s Datebook said it was in a log cabin.)
Birthplace: December 15 (NBC didn't give a year, but it was 1949)
Hair: Sandy
Eyes: Blue
Marital Status: Single
Residence: Santa Monica, Calif.

That kind of stuff certainly doesn't give a valid description of the man who shapes and creates mysteriously sizzling Sonny Crockett on *Miami Vice*.

An old interview and some clippings tell Don's story in his own words. While a Datebook article out of L.A. described him as the grandson of a preacher man in an Ozark country church named Hornybuck, Don's ver-

sion of events is much more explicit. (The article was headlined "A Real-Life Rake as a Revolutionary Rogue" and it promoted *The Rebels*, a mini-series he co-starred in. To promote the same show, a public relations agency said that Don would love to become a cross between Montgomery Clift and Gary Cooper, which plenty of women think he's doing in *Miami Vice*!)

Don described his grandfather's church: "Some people like to call it Holy Rollers. When I was four or five, I would get up and sing 'Rock of Ages,' and then they'd come up afterwards and pinch me on the cheek, give me a quarter and say, 'Isn't that cute?' and everything. So right then and there I'm sure I got the show business bug."

Questioned in later years about the *Datebook* story, he said "That's somebody's clever copy...I never said that. I always sort of had a feeling that I would be in some form of the entertainment business, such as sports..."

At the age of 11, Don's parents divorced. "I had a terrific childhood...[it's traumatic] when a stable seemingly stable family falls...You're never ready for it. No, it was a sudden thing. You know it turned me

Lusty and hell raising, Judson Fletcher in MCA TV/Universal's The Rebels.

"I had a disciplinary problem at school. I think like anyone who is inventive. I wasn't really a criminal, I was inventive."

around quite a bit because I was at the age where I was just starting to open my eyes about male/female relationships. It's a critical age. That's one of the reasons I went bad and I was a juvenile delinquent."

What turned him around? "The judge telling me that I would spend the rest of my days until I was 18 years old in a home for boys. That did it. I can't stand confinement of any type. I had a disciplinary problem at school. I think like anyone who is inventive. I wasn't really a criminal, I was inventive. I could think up things to do that were ornery and mischievous."

The experience wound up as a lyric he wrote for Dickey Betts of the Allman Brothers band, the hit, "Can't Take it With You."

"That's part of my youth...I stole a car when I was 12 and got arrested. That's the second line [of the song]. I went to a boy's farm for about two weeks, and that's when I had to go live with my father. 'At that time of life,' it goes, 'hot wire fast car just to take a ride, you can run, but you sure cannot hide.'

"I met Dickey when I was working on *Return to Macon County*. We were shooting out in front of his driveway and he couldn't get out. Finally, he got pissed off, as Southern boys will do, and drove right through the scene. Afterwards, I happened to recognize his truck down at the local liquor store, and I said, 'Aren't you the guy who just did that?' and he said 'Yeah.' And I said, 'Well, I'm pleased to meet anybody who would do that. Who are you?' 'Dickey Betts,' he says. '*The* Dickey Betts?' 'Yeah.'

"We started out talking and we talked for three-and-a-half hours non-stop. We had just gone through a whole catharsis that ended with us cracking up for a half hour. From that time on we've been fast friends."

The song, which so touched on his childhood, was written while they were on the road somewhere, drunk in a bar, talking about "life and love and the pursuit of happiness."

Don remembered, "It came out of that, and then I'd forgotten about it. Dickey called me six or eight months later, and I was sitting up at the house and he says, 'Hey, Listen! I'm kicking this around and can't do anything with it. Why don't you see what you can do?' I was feeling kinda depressed, and he told me it was 'Can't Take It With You.' I said alright and got off the phone with him, and then minutes later, while I was kicking the line around my head, I went right to a piece of paper and pencil and I wrote down three verses just as if you were sitting here dictating."

His first real involvement with show business came at the age of 12. He did Midwest night clubs as favors. "I had a little act, where I stood up by the piano player and I would do a little tap dance and stuff like that. My mother was basically responsible for that. I needed some extra money and so she knew this friend (it happened as a fluke) who had a club. In Kansas they have private clubs because it's a dry state. We can drink, but you have to have your liquor card and pay a membership fee to a private club. It's really bizarre. I could sing there without being underage, because you couldn't drink.

"I would make $30-$40 a week. To me, at that time, $30-$40 a week under the table was Wow! Cash! Singing in a club...who cares about that? I said I'd do it for my mother's friends and then I would sing at a wedding reception. It was strange, once it got started, it started pyramiding. And when I was at college, I was driving 32 miles to Kansas City and singing in the piano bar of a hotel lounge."

Athletics was something Don had to give up when he fell into acting.

"I was taking a business class when I was in high school. It was business administration. (He was working nights.) I couldn't stay awake in class. I fell asleep in there from the first day to the third day and then the teacher threw me out. So I went to the counselor and I told her about this little mishap and she said, 'Well, the only class open is a dramatics class and you'll have to forget about your athletics.'

"I was into football at the time and she said I'd have to forget about athletics because it's a conflict with this particular thing. I needed a credit to graduate and I didn't want to stay at school. She told me I needed to ask the teacher permission to take the class. So I went to the drama teacher and asked her, and she asked me, 'Can you sing?' 'Yeah, I can sing.' I would have told her anything. I would have told her I could juggle if it would help. She said, 'Alright. Be at the auditions tonight at around 4 p.m.'

"I didn't know what she was talking about, so I went to the auditorium about 4 p.m. and I sang for her. She gave me a script to read. I looked it over and then I read. She said 'O.K., you've got the part (Tony in *West Side Story*) and you're in the class.' During that time I started doing plays in semi-professional theatre. Until then, I was basically a singer in my grandfather's church.

"I sometimes look back on it and think, Jesus, I wish...I wanted to be a wide receiver so bad, and I was a good wide receiver. And sometimes when I'm sitting at home watching football, I think 'damn it!' "

Don left home for good at the age of 15. With his background in theatre work, what he was doing in high school and in semi-professional productions, he was noticed by scouts from the University of Kansas Drama school as a very effective Starbuck in *The Rainmaker*, and offered a rare full scholarship.

After a year and a half at the University of Kansas he was noticed by Ed Hastings of the American Conservatory Theatre of San Francisco (ACT) in *Rake's Progress*. Ed was in town to direct an operetta for the school when he spotted Don, and simultaneously, Don's favorite professor (so favorite he lived with her from the age of 15), who was subsequently hired by ACT. "At that age I still needed a mother, but kind of crossed the boundaries a little bit.

"It worked out perfectly. Four days before the semester was up the dean had said to me, 'Well, you have two choices. You can quit or we can throw you out.' So I packed my stuff and went to San Francisco." He was 18 at the time.

Recalling his introduction to Los Angeles and the magic world of Hollywood, Don tells the following story:

"I started in this town cold. I was at ACT in San Francisco. I was studying with them, as well as being part of the company. I was 18 and Sal Mineo was doing *Fortune and Men's Eyes*. I heard about it and it was a terrific role for a young actor. It was powerful and demanding...almost too demanding. I ended up doing it for eight months.

"But when I first heard about it, I sent him a picture and a resume and he said I looked reasonably right for the part. He called me and asked me if I would like to come down and audition for him. Well, absolutely! So I got on a plane and showed up in L.A. on October 31, Halloween, 1968.

"I was apprehensive about taking a big step into the big city. I mean it's all or nothing. It can kill you, you know, let's put the old life on the line."

In fact, Sal Mineo had gone through 500 actors and couldn't find what he wanted until Don came to L.A.

"I wanted to be a wide receiver so bad, and I was a good wide receiver."

"I really looked innocent, but I had the strength to carry out the character because he was a virile, strong character. (It was a prison drama, very explicit, with nude scenes...and in the role, Don gets raped in the shower.) So I flew down and auditioned and Sal said, 'You've got the role. You were terrific, you'll be great.'"

Don recalls, "My family was being put through the mill with my career because I was an innovator in a lot of things. *Fortune* was the first time there was a graphic rape scene that took place on stage and it involved a certain amount of nudity. It was avant garde and they had to deal with a lot of things.

"I hope to God I would have the strength, the patience and understanding that my parents have had with me over the years. They are basically very much Southern conservative...well, they are liberal in their wisdom. Their wise wisdom creates a liberalism which goes hand in hand with very high social and personal morals.

"I had never even seen *Rebel Without a Cause* until after I met Sal Mineo, but I was impressed with him because he was a total gentleman. There I was, 18 years old, and I'd been a professional for already three or four years. I still had horse---- on my boots.

"Sal was probably one of the best infuences on my career or on my acting, because Sal was a fine actor. He did a lot of s--tty movies. He would have said so himself. But he was highly underrated. He won two Academy Award nominations, one when he was 15 or 16 years old. And you know, that's one of the things that I have a slight bitterness about this business.

"Sal is a perfect example of someone who grew out of himself, out of the characters he portrayed, and the town just forgot about him. He was exceptional, he had great taste and style. He was very real and very strong, regardless of the stories that travelled around town. He was a very strong individual and one of the most generous men I have ever met.

"He was a great asset to my career and advised me a great deal on how to deal with certain things in the business. We were good friends and we kept in touch the whole time. I saw him four days before he was killed...I went off to Columbia, California to work on the film *The Law of the Land*, and my sister called me. It was a shock. A total shock. That type of thing you never really get over."

One of the earliest records of Don's professional career in that old, creaky filing cabinet came from a 1970 *L.A. Herald Examiner* piece headlined, "Don Johnson, Searching For Identity" from the Associated Press wire services. He was described as a "young Greek God."

Those who are too young to remember just how wild the 1970s were, should know those were the days when the potheads reigned supreme, college campuses were hotbeds of rebellion and experimentation, the sexual revolution was in full swing, and no one really cared about Greek gods. Except Don Johnson was not an ordinary Greek god and was starring in a movie which dealt precisely with all of the above... *The Magic Garden of Stanley Sweetheart.*

"I identify with him," said Don in the 1970 interview. He was only 19 when he made the movie and it became clear he was telling the truth. Would you call it typecasting if you were told that he was arraigned by the Beverly Hills police for smoking pot?

Fifteen years later, Don was going to become a national sweetheart as a *Miami Vice* detective on network TV, with a 1985 Emmy nomination for "Best Actor in a Dramatic Series." (The award went to veteran

The Magic Garden of Stanley Sweetheart–Don was only 19 when he made this MGM Movie.

A 1985 Emmy nomination for "Best Actor in a Dramatic Series" as Detective Crockett in Miami Vice.

actor William Daniels for his role in *St. Elsewhere*, a realistic hospital show.)

But even as a 19-year-old, Don's intelligence and introspection became obvious when he interpreted his first leading role in a major movie:

"Stanley Sweetheart represents all of us, or maybe a particular time in our lives. What Stanley is doing is making a place in a society that's just monstrous. It's lonely, man. You try to decide…Am I a student, a filmmaker, a writer, a construction worker? What happens to him (Stanley) is what happens when kids are confused. They start playing different roles like Brando or a super-hippie to see what fits…"

Later in his life, when questioned about Stanley by an interviewer who felt that he was explaining the role in terms of himself, Don responded:

"I don't think I was doing that at all. I think that I was saying that he was representative of most everyone's feelings at that time, not just mine. He was a college student. You probably didn't see the film…because about two people did. I think outside of myself, it may have been my mother.

"Stanley was going through the same type of cathar-

sis that everybody was going through at that time. The Viet Nam War. The search for who am I. What am I doing here? What we are all doing all the time. It was just one of those films that was taken advantage of by studio executives and exploited. It was unfortunate for the film, because it had a lot of content."

While the film was being made by MGM, the giant studio had three different Presidents, all of whom changed the film in some way or another. "Each time a new President took over, a new regime would happen, they would take all the stuff from the President before and say, 'that's crap.' You know, they didn't care about the film. They just wanted their record to look clean, which is usually the case with the executive positions when it concerns creative material that they know basically nothing about."

It was certainly an education for Don, who admits it was the beginning of disillusionment. "I was led to believe I was starring in a major motion picture. But there weren't any at that time. Everything was low budget. They were trying to make it for a million bucks (that's less than each episode of *Miami Vice* costs!) on the streets of New York. We didn't even have dressing rooms. We dressed in the back of prop trucks, in the cafe we were shooting in, or in men's rooms... wherever we were. It was shot on the run in New York City and we were dodging permit inspectors. It was a joke the way that movie was made."

You certainly cannot say that the Miami or Dade County permit inspectors are chasing the cast of *Miami Vice* around town. In fact, Don and his partner, Philip Michael Thomas, were awarded keys to the city and police from the Metro Dade police department, who, in addition to being consultants to the show, are sometimes in it.

In the early '70s Don also did a film called *The Harrad Experiment*, which was successful with college students. It depicted a college campus where professors and students were experimenting with Free Love. Life following fiction, at the age of 22, Don ran off with Tippy Hedren's (*The Birds*) 14-year-old daughter, Melanie Griffith, who was in the film with him. Their love connection and marriage lasted four years.

In 1979, Don claimed that there was no parallel between two college dropouts. Stanley was finding himself through drugs, sex and fantasies.

In 1985, reformed and finely-honed for *Miami Vice*, Don admits he was always looking for the next party. "I never drank or did drugs while I was working," quoted an article in *People* Magazine. "But brother, when they said wrap, I would try to set the land speed record.

"There are always little things you want to change about yourself, you know," Don said a while back. "I have an incredible amount of discipline and will-power when I want it, when I must have it. But I had no discipline for my discipline... in other words, I didn't use it enough. I guess you could say I was either a fool or extremely confident or both.

"I guess I've always had pretty much confidence, and I've been rather confident and cocky at times ... maybe even a real smartass and arrogant. I don't really think it's a healthy attitude, but I don't think it's unhealthy, unless you're just selfish and mindless about other people. If you're inconsiderate, then it can be detrimental, but I'm not that way."

It's not easy for him to forget the excesses which almost destroyed his career. His girlfriend, Patti D'Arbanville, and their son, Jesse (who was three in December '85), have given him the first happy family life he's ever had, turning him around with the help of what Don calls "a higher power."

"Patti is my best friend. I trust her implicitly. She unconditionally cares about me and I about her. We have obvious problems that come from any kind of relationship, only ours are a little more public. But one reason we're able to maintain our relationship is that we are not married. A lot of times, in a marriage, you end up living someone else's idea of what it's supposed to be like, some storybook thing. As I've said about partying, I've partied. I've also been married."

Nancy Reagan invited Don and Patti to the White House in September of '85, because she wants to enlist him in her national anti-drug campaign. "We were treated like royalty. The President kept smiling and winking at Jesse. Right at the place they do the security check, Jesse kept looking at the Secret Service guys. When he saw one of their guns, he turned around and said loudly, 'Daddy, did you bring your gun?' I said, 'Shussh, shussh.' The Secret Service

Don Johnson pictured here with 3-year-old son Jesse at the Live Aid concert in Philadelphia, June '85.

Patty D'Arbanville and Don Johnson partying with John Taylor and Andy Taylor at the Area nightclub in New York City.

computer printout sheets and profit margins. Leave the creativity to the professionals. Too much of the time I think that the business is dollar conscious as opposed to quality conscious. I believe that if you have quality you make the film uncompromisingly as possible...You all know making a film is a series of compromises, but the fewer the compromises, the better the film. I believe that."

The film for which he won "Best Actor" from the Science Fiction Academy was called *A Boy and His Dog*, written by the famous writer, Harlan Ellison. (Harlan also did some *Star Trek* scripts.) The futurist movie takes place after a nuclear devastation, when there's very little food around and a man can't survive without his dog. At the end of the movie, would you believe that Don Johnson feeds his girlfriend to his dog?

The Jefferson Davis Prewitt role in NBC's *From Here to Eternity*, was his first TV role. He even managed to incorporate his musical talents into it. "I've always wanted to do *From Here to Eternity*. I mean, ever since I saw Montgomery Clift in the origi-

With Patty at the Emmys in Pasadena.

guys were getting nervous but the President and the First Lady fell in love with him. Jesse had a ball.

"I mean, let's face it. There we were, all three of us, holding hands and playing '1-2-3 jump' in the halls of The White House. President Reagan asked me to autograph the *Miami Vice Time* cover."

Patti recalled dancing after dinner for the Ambassador from Denmark: "Donnie and I looked around and into each others eyes and said, 'I love you.' We had come so far."

According to Don, the making of *The Magic of Stanley Sweetheart*, which he did after *Fortune and Men's Eyes*, didn't help his career. "It was more detrimental to me at that time than anything else. If it hadn't been for the film I did after that, *Zaccariah* (a rock western), I had a hard time getting work. Even then it was difficult, because it was classified as grade C trash and my validity as an actor went right out the window. They weren't taking the time they used to to take with the stars of the old days. These days, you have to design your presentation of yourself to the executives."

After his experience with *The Magic Garden of Stanley Sweetheart*, Don went on record and declared, "I would take the creative control out of the hands of the businessmen and I would let them stick with their

44

The group Power Station, feeling Don's beard at the Area nightclub.

nal and when I knew they were making the mini-series, I wanted desperately to do it.

"I think there's a great deal of art in television, but you just have to work harder and dig deeper to find it. In bits and pieces, here and there you find it. Sometimes you get lucky [the way he did with *Miami Vice*]. Quality suffers a great deal, but TV is still a very powerful medium. TV is too big to stay out of and it's too powerful to ignore."

Don's early opinion of censorship was to the point and hasn't changed. Referring to attempts to censor *Fortune and Men's Eyes* and *The Magic Garden of Stanley Sweetheart* he declared, "In a kind of way it's an indirect lie. It appears to be a sheltering of people from things that really happen. My job is to create and portray a character of life..."

That's definitely what he's doing in his role in *Miami Vice*. Defending the violence and scenes in the show which cause ulcers at the Broadcast Standards Bureau, Don declared "The violence in our show is not gratuitous. It occurs in direct response to threats on the lives of police officers or citizens, or in the line of police work."

Describing the people he works with on *Miami Vice*,

Don said, "This is the most unselfish group of actors I've ever worked with. We're a bunch of misfits, really. Everyone of these people has paid his dues. The only thing that really makes us feel good is to take these chances. We've been through drugs and alcohol and outlaws and thieves. The whole crew is reformed. I mean, we've really been around the block. I'm not saying that we're the only messiah of the street, but we're damned sure one of them.

"I've had some terrific people throughout my life who were kind enough to share with me their understanding and knowledge of certain things I didn't know about, coming from the part of the country that I come from. You don't grow up around all this. You don't know it. There's a different set of values and a different set of morals, a different set of business rules, how to handle business.

"Where I come from, a man's word is his word, and you know, that's what I believe. When you say you are going to do something, then you do it. So much of the time in this business, people don't work on their word or even contracts. It's as if contracts were made to be broken. There's not a contract in this town that is binding. Not one. Not a contract in town. We see it time

Detectives Crockett and Tubbs storm a hideout in "Cool Runnin' " Miami Vice.

and time again."

What's the best part of working on *Miami Vice*?

"I like a role that has good structure, with nothing filled in. Then I can create the characters within the author's boundaries, but I don't like to nail things down. I'd rather suggest than spell everything out. I want the audience to become involved with me, to work with me as I develop the character. Well rounded defined roles I've played are not necessarily me. They have a part of me and I work within and from my own experiences."

That's exactly what he does in the show. It's been noted that points on the show are made through gestures, looks, music and artful composition. In one episode, Sonny is so involved with his new girlfriend that Rico got into trouble when Sonny didn't show up on time. They don't even talk to each other.

All the necessary communication is done when they exchange looks of recrimination and guilt. They only speak to each other at the very end of the show...as they walk off arm in arm and decide to go fishing.

The things Don said about TV years ago are obviously the things he still believes. And it becomes clear, when one watches *Miami Vice* that he has found the ideal working environment for his style of acting and the standards of quality he set for himself.

Expressing some dissatisfaction with one episode of *Miami Vice* he says, "Here's the thing. Our show will never be the same every week. Which is one of the reasons I love it. We don't have a formula. The problem is trying to tell the story from beginning to middle to end in an hour without losing the human aspect. The character bits and studies. The relationships."

When questioned about the fact he plays the macho leader of the salt and pepper undercover team, he responds frankly: "After all, what we're doing is selling soap. And a major proportion that buys is white. And they have to relate. On the other hand, we're stretching the boundaries as far as we can stretch them."

Sometimes compromising quality can get to you. According to Don, it does, sometimes. "But you learn

A grim-faced Detective Crockett coiled for action in "The Home Invaders" Miami Vice.

Don Johnson at an NBC press conference at the Visage nightclub, New York City.

Does he need a shave? Don Johnson, Visage nightclub, June 1985.

how to handle that. You learn how to be prepared and do your homework and you have it ready. The only way I have ever done anything in this business was by being a little bit sharper, a little bit more prepared and a little bit better than some of the others. I grew up in this business. I was a baby in it, and TV was appealing, because at least I was working and the only way in my mind you become an actor is to work and perfect your craft. To constantly take the chances and go for it.

"I certainly didn't get into the business with a family name like a lot of people in the business whose parents were in it. This industry is like any other business, you know. It's like banking, lawyers, doctors. I basically cracked it in my own way, without ever going into contract to one specific studio for more than one situation. It's difficult to do that and retain any sense of dignity about it."

Until *Miami Vice*, Don felt strongly that in a TV series you couldn't grow as an actor. Years ago he said, "There comes a point where you say, yeah, well, I

have two choices. I can be either a total and complete artist and stay the hell out of the film business altogether and do theatre and be a full out and out artist and live in hovels.

"You can't make enough money as a legitimate actor to sustain any kind of living. You have to work two or three jobs at once. So you end up making a decision.... Do I reach this many people and have at least some sort of reasonable living? Or do I concentrate and forget about that and exist within my purity as an actor. That's all fine and good, but that doesn't put food in your mouth and it gets really hungry out there."

For years he did all sorts of different things, so he could try different materials. One of the things he felt kept him from being recognizably famous in his Holly-wood years was the fact that he may have done impressive roles, but that he was so totally locked into the characters, you couldn't see the real Don Johnson shine through.

Now Don's presence is commanding. He's cool on the surface, totally involved in his work, stretching himself to the limit, pushing and pushing at the boundaries. His silver blue Mercedes is parked outside a modern trailer. No more men's rooms and prop trucks for him. The good looks, those incredible eyes and that sexual vulnerability keep millions home on Friday nights. Sonny Crockett has been described as a "boiling pot of emotions that are most often discharged in wiseass smart talk. But the love hurt ex-husband and devoted dad peek through those sad eyes and drive

One of the coolest announcers at the Live Aid concert in Philadelphia.

A night out in "The Big Apple" with girlfriend Patty.

"It's absolutely magic how everything works out."

Arriving for a post-Emmy dinner, at Spago restaurant in West Hollywood.

the girls wild."

Don thought he was already successful when he went to San Francisco 17 years ago. Now he's working harder than ever to have enough latitude to run his own film company. "Like everyone else, I don't think anyone can do it as well as I can. I look back and realize that although I've struggled for years, it ain't over yet. In fact, it's just beginning. First you struggle to get money, then you struggle to keep it. Then you struggle to get quality into the work you do and keep that. You can make a living and not see your artistic values go down the tubes. But it's all compromise. You can never expect to get exactly what you want, you can only hope to get close."

Years ago Don declared: "I think it's total magic, I really do. It's absolutely magic how everything works out. The way life in general works out, it's magical, but in this business I think it's magic that you can make movies at all and the fact that I'm part of making them is magic, it's poetry in motion. It's almost like my life is like a flying carpet ride, it's a wonderful world of constant amazement!"

For now, *Miami Vice* is Don's magic carpet, and he's riding it into a dynamite, fantastic future.

"It's a lot of pressure to live up to the high mark we've set for ourselves. But it's a joy to have your peers enjoy your work. I've never had anything that's had an effect like this in 17 years in the business."

EDWARD JAMES OLMOS
AND THE SUPPORTING CAST

Edward James Olmos, the granite Lieutenant Martin Castillo of *Miami Vice*, won an Emmy in 1985 for best supporting actor in a dramatic series, after just one season. When he accepted it, he was torn between the tragedy of the Mexico City earthquake, which had just happened, and the exuberance and joy of the moment of victory. "Yeah, he does smile." His character, Lt. Castillo, is a no-nonsense type whose mere entrance into a room can charge it with an electrified air of mystery and foreboding.

"I hope the character of Castillo will stay rooted enough in his own reality to pass the test of time," says Olmos of the character he plays.

Castillo replaced Lt. Rodriquez during *Miami Vice*'s first season. He's the counterpoint to the fashionable pastels favored by his cohorts. In regulation black suit and white shirt, complete with narrow tie, he carries a grim visage and never makes small talk. We hear the synthesizer music crank up when he appears. His words are spare and to the point: "Let's take care of business," adding a classic western hero touch to the show. Shades of *Shane*.

"One of the things I have found most exciting about *Miami Vice* is that they have allowed me to play this character the way I wanted to play him. Castillo is very disciplined, very obsessive in his routines. He is a Ninja warrior. In order to be a very good combatant of crime, you have to understand crime. So Castillo walks a very thin line."

"We've discussed Castillo's private life at great length," volunteers Don Johnson. "We make jokes about it all the time. My favorite thing is to do a Castillo. (He demonstrates.) You walk up to a wall, face two inches away, put your hands in your pockets, don't blink, don't smile, and say very directly, "Find them." Eddie Olmos has the character down so well, he doesn't have to talk anymore. All he has to do is look..."

Philip Michael Thomas says that people are amazed that Eddie Olmos is so friendly off-screen. "At home Castillo probably sits in the Zen position, puts on a kamikaze headband, lights candles and chants. I've never met a cop remotely like him."

In one episode, Sonny and Rico offer to help out the

Edward James Olmos, the granite Lieutenant Martin Castillo of Miami Vice.

Tight-lipped Detectives Crockett and Tubbs in "Score, Part 1" Miami Vice.

Lieutenant and even a score from his mysterious past. A powerful Chinese opium chieftain arrives in Miami and dares him to subvert his massive narcotics shipment by kidnapping Castillo's missing wife—who thinks her husband is dead.

Castillo, who spent years in Thailand working for the U.S. Drug Enforcement Agency, had many of his men ambushed and slaughtered by General Lao Ti, the suddenly visible drug warlord. The tormented Castillo knows that his wife is in enemy hands, and has to act accordingly.

Olmos further describes the character, "He's much more conservative than either Crockett or Tubbs. He doesn't want to draw attention to himself. He is a man who can come in and not be noticed, so that he can study the situation around him. The less you know, the more you want to find out. He has a sensitivity and a passion, yet is distant. That arouses the need to know more about him."

A native of East Los Angeles, Olmos has taken pains

to keep the Castillo figure cloaked in secrecy on and off the screen. He figures that less is more.

Like Don Johnson and Philip Michael Thomas, Eddie Olmos is no newcomer to show business. He was nominated for a Tony for his 1978 performance in the stage musical *Zoot Suit*, which also earned him a Drama Critic's Circle Award, and the role in the film.

Eddie began performing as a teenager when he formed his own musical group, playing to sellout audiences. For the next 14 years, he honed his acting skills in L.A.'s experimental theatre. He's done the prerequisite series appearances on TV and produced, financed and directed *The Ballad of Gregorio Cortez*, a critically acclaimed feature film.

"People are starting to take a harder look at what Castillo's all about," said Olmos. "That will only help in the long run. Most people only know me as Castillo because they haven't seen any of my other work.

He sees the recent successes of Miami Vice *as the result of the chemistry between leads Johnson and Thomas.*

Olivia Brown with Philip Michael Thomas.

Castillo is rooted in a by-the-book way of dealing with problems that doesn't apply to Crockett and Tubbs. They're more explosive, but between the three of us, we achieve a balance."

The Olmos family moved to Miami when his part became a permanent one. He sees the recent successes of *Miami Vice* as the result of the chemistry between leads Johnson and Thomas. "Another factor is the storytelling. It's gotten better since the early shows, and we've hit paydirt because of it."

Olmos concludes, "To be honest, I don't know what will happen specifically. but in the real world times are getting worse, not better. I see it in the Miami papers every day. There are bigger and bigger vice busts. Things are not slowing down around here, and that will probably be reflected in the show."

OLIVIA BROWN

Olivia Brown, who once played a heroin-addicted snitch for three episodes of *Hill Street Blues*, plays Trudy Joplin, back-up detective for Crockett and Tubbs. Born in Frankfurt, Germany, the eldest daughter of a criminal lawyer, she grew up in Sacramento and thought she would be an interior decorator. As a

child, she worked in a local theatre and in 1975, she won a national stand-up comedy contest.

The lady enjoys just being on the set of *Miami Vice*. "I know it may sound silly, but at first, everything amazed me. Lots of people find bad things in the business, but I don't. At the stars' network affiliate party, I wanted to walk around with an autograph book. I even send the visitor's passes from the studio lots to my sister. She collects them."

Olivia had roles in *Streets of Fire*, and Eddie Murphy's *48 HRS*. She has done guest shots on *The Loveboat*, *For Love and Honor*, and *T.J. Hooker*.

Positive roles like Trudy Joplin's *Miami Vice* don't show up very often on TV series, and Olivia says really glad to get it: "My role is that of an intelligent black woman with street sense."

Olivia is married to actor Mykel T. Williamson, who predicted their nuptuals when they met at an audition. "I had no intention of getting married," said Olivia. "I wanted to be a kind of international playgirl. Now I'm more of an international wife."

MICHAEL TALBOTT

He doesn't wear Armani suits, drive Ferraris or get into the magazines like fellow actors Don Johnson and Philip Michael Thomas, but Mike Talbott, who plays Detective Switek, has his share of fans.

In Miami's stylish Coconut Grove neighborhood, he's the self-designated and unofficial mayor.

"I gave myself that title," said Mike, "I know all the people in the Grove. I live there, too. I don't tell them, but they know I'm the mayor. That entitles me to executive privileges, such as good seating, and they know I'll tip heavily."

As a kid, the Iowa-born Talbott was hanging out at the local gas station when he was spotted by the high school's new drama teacher, who encouraged him to go into acting. "I got more interested in plays as a

Director Paul Michael Glaser (2nd from left) goes over upcoming scene on Miami Vice.

Lt. Rodriguez (Gregory Sierra), pictured at left with Crockett and Tubbs, was replaced during the first season by Lieutenant Martin Castillo (Edward James Olmos).

The main cast of Miami Vice.

sophomore," said Mike. "As a senior, I realized I could make people laugh, so I decided to make it in acting." Otherwise he would have become "a heavy equipment operator, a law enforcement officer or a Marine Corps general."

He did make it. He's been in movies: *First Blood*, *Bloodsport*, and Michael Mann's *Thief*. He's also done guest spots on a number of TV shows, including *Amber Waves* and *A Death in Canaan*.

Although his outfits are a far cry from the wardrobes provided for Don and Philip, Michael and his partner, John Diehl, get to wear loud floral prints, and he describes the ensembles as "sweaty." "I don't like polyester, but I like the cotton and the golf shoes. I'd say our budget for clothes is about six bucks. If I had anything to say about it, I'd be wearing shorts."

After an episode in which he and John Diehl were prominently featured, he began getting fan mail. "People were writing to say they were glad we got our shot. Of course, they always sign it, 'Your Number One Fan.'

"My character is a lot like me. I like to keep spirits high by joking around. I don't use much caution in my humor; I like to do everything in extremes. I am still a little crazy and wild. On the set, I like to tell people someone is looking for them...drives 'em nuts. My maid thinks my humor is funny, but then, she doesn't speak English."

While Don Johnson and Philip Michael Thomas grace magazine covers all over the country, Mike's ambition is to be on the cover of just one: *Mad Magazine*. It's the kind of literature he enjoys reading.

JOHN DIEHL

It was after John Diehl was noticed as a crazy radical in the movie *Leon's Case*, that he was hired as Detective Larry Zito in *Miami Vice*. Describing the role, John says, "He's very conscientious, but he's so gung-ho, he messes up, like a cat that lives through distemper...spastic and ungraceful."

A former used-car salesman in Amsterdam, Holland, John traveled around the world for 10 years. "From 1966 to 1976, I went through a period to get in

TV's hottest undercover detectives at a press conference in New York City.

touch with myself." Born in Cincinnati, he recalls "I'm always doing that, but those 10 years were remarkable because I was like a blank page. It was my period of non-ness."

Truck driver, orderly, house painter and bartender. The jobs he took before he was inspired to become an actor contrasted with the jobs he had after his sister urged him to go into acting. He started out doing lighting in a local play, and was soon taking voice lessons. He's had roles on *Hill Street*, and was in the films *Escape From New York*, *D.C. Cab*, and *Stripes*.

SAUNDRA SANTIAGO

Like other crew members in *Miami Vice*, Saundra Santiago, who plays Detective Gina Navarro, was a late bloomer in dramatics. "I think I had always wanted to act somewhere in the back of my mind, but never dared. The product of a strict Catholic upbringing, I kept thinking, 'I'm a Catholic and nice Catholic girls simply don't go off to become actresses.

"Other people love to talk of what acting is all about. I'm basically a shy person. I do my work and go home. I don't party outside the job. I'm most comfortable being home with my friends and family."

Born in The Bronx, Saundra and her family moved to Miami when she was 12. She graduated from the University of Miami with a Bachelor's Degree in Fine Arts and then studied theatre at Methodist University in Dallas. After getting her Master's Degree, she took off for New York and played Catherine in *A View From the Bridge* on Broadway. Her movie credits include *Beat Street*, which was released in the summer of 1985.

"As for my character, concludes Saundra, "I see her as being pretty sensitive, with a sense of humor. On the other hand, she's emotional and definitely not a wimp. I'm a little more talkative."